GUINNESS THE GOOD GIRL

Guinness

the Good Girl

™

DEDICATION

....

....

....

....

....

....

GUINNESS
THE GOOD GIRL™

written by
MATTHEW GILLMANN

illustrated by
PENNY WEBER

When Dottie turned eight, her parents told her she could finally get her biggest wish – a puppy named Guinness.

"Guinness is going to be a Dalmatian," said Dottie.

"I've heard Dalmatians can be a lot of trouble," said her father, Dewey.

"Guinness won't be trouble," said Dottie. "She's going to be a good girl!"

"You can have a Dalmatian if you earn straight A's at school this semester," said her mother, Rocelia. "You will also have to save 50 big ones for a dog license from the city."

"Done deal," said Dottie. She started saving coins in her piggy bank and she did all of her homework. When her report card arrived, Dottie had all A's.

Tune Town School
Report Card

Reading Ⓐ
Writing Ⓐ
Math Ⓐ
History Ⓐ
Language Ⓐ
Geography Ⓐ

Dottie found a place called Daphne's Dal House. Their two Dalmatians called Little Miss Can't Do Wrong and Sir DoRight were expecting puppies.

I'm certain they will have some nice puppies, thought Dottie. She and her parents placed the order.

Daphne's

DabHouse

After the puppies were born, Dottie learned that her puppy was named Nothin' but Trouble! That did not seem like a good sign, but Rocelia said she could change the name to Guinness.

Your puppy – Nothin' but Trouble!

When little Guinness arrived,
the first thing Dottie noticed
was her heart shaped nose.
"I knew you would have a
good heart, Guinness,
but I wasn't
expecting two!"

In truth, Guinness
was a little bit of
trouble at first.

Soon though, Guinness was acting like a
good girl and even learned some tricks.

"Biscuit roll!" said Dottie.

One day Rocelia told Dottie that Guinness had reached the age when she needed a license, since the city keeps tracks of all dogs.

"You'll need to go downtown with those 50 big ones you have been saving," said Rocelia.

When Dottie got her piggy bank, she found there was no way to get the coins out. Its only opening was the thin slot for inserting the coins. She set it down, not sure what to do next.

Suddenly, Guinness jumped
onto the coffee table.

The piggy bank crashed onto the floor, breaking into pieces.

"That's one way to get the coins out. Good girl, Guinness!"

Dottie and Guinness rushed
to downtown Tune Town.

When Dottie and Guinness arrived downtown, they saw a crowd on the streets, watching a burning building.

The fire truck could not get through.

Dottie saw the fire fighters trying to turn on the siren and blow the horn, but they didn't make a sound. They must have been broken.

Suddenly, Guinness ran off.

"Oh no!" Dottie wondered
what Guinness could be up to.

Guinness ran in front of
the fire truck and barked.
The crowds looked at
Guinness and the fire truck and
hurried out of the way. Guinness led the fire
truck through the crowds to the burning building.

After the fire was out, the President of Earl & Roth Enterprises gave Guinness a prize.

"It is with pleasure and gratitude that I present to you our latest product, tap dancing shoes for dogs."

Then Tune Town's fire chief named Guinness
Honorary Fire Dog of Tune Town.

"Guinness, you're a true fire dog!"
shouted the chief.

TUNE TOW

Dottie and Guinness finally arrived at City Hall and went inside.

"Are you the license man?" asked Dottie.

"Yes! They call me Dan the License Man. Do you have 50 big ones?"

Dottie dropped all the coins from the piggy bank on the counter.

"Oh . . . that looks like a lot of little ones! I'll go get my friend, Stan, to help count."

"Are you Stan the License
Man?" asked Dottie.

"They call me Stan the Muscle Man . . ."

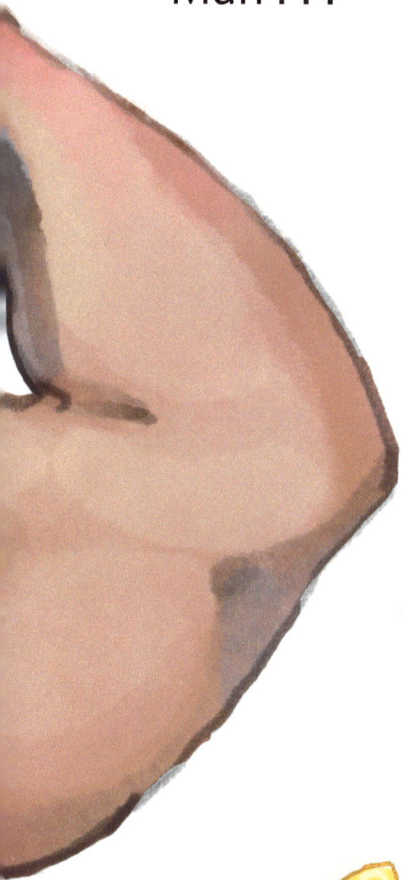

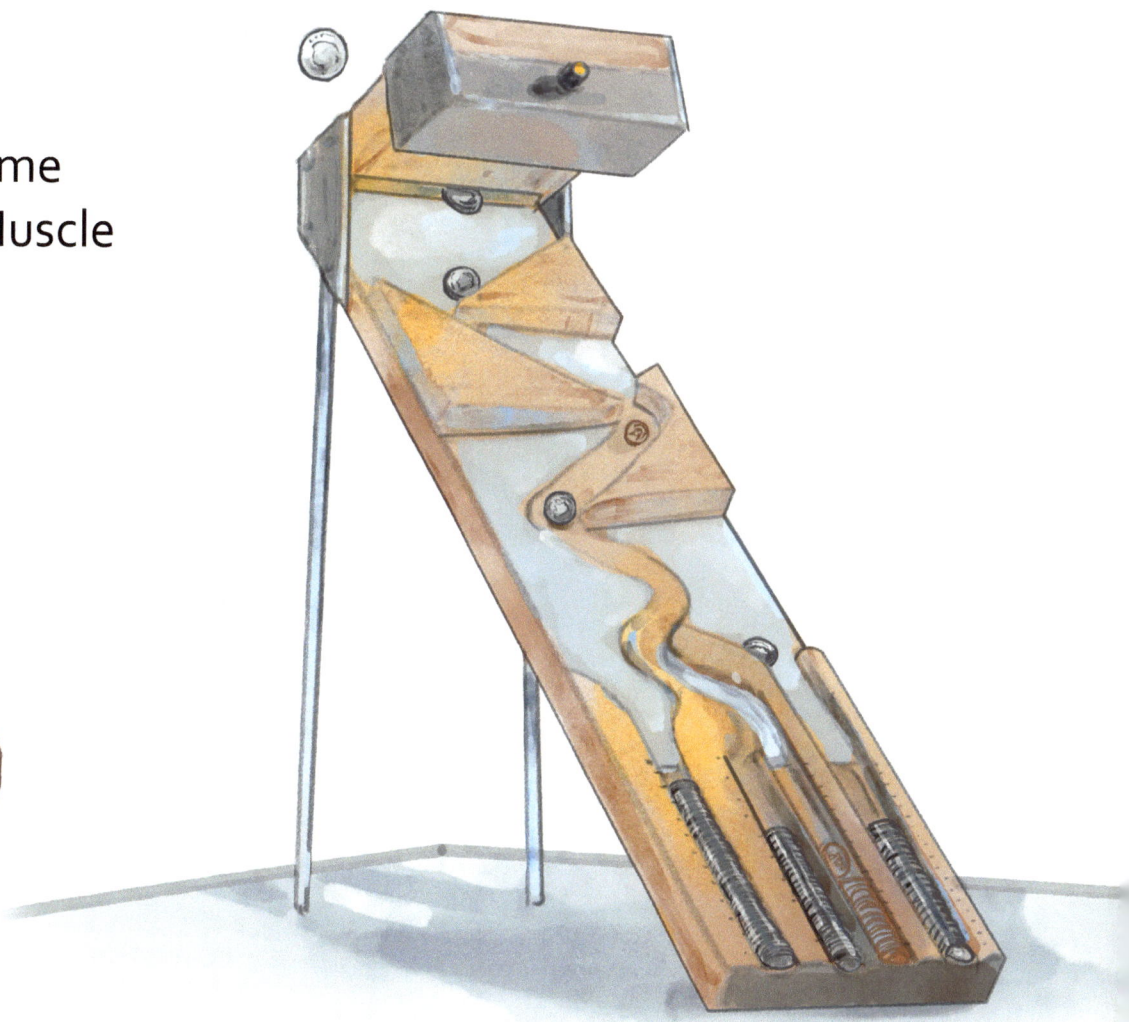

" . . . but I'm also the man with the plan. We can use my handy dandy coin counting contraption."

"What's your puppy's name?" asked Dan.

"Guinness the Good Girl," said Dottie.

Soon Dan and Stan were hanging Guinness's license around her neck.

Dottie said, "Now you're officially . . .

...GUINNESS THE GOOD GIRL!"

SPOTTY DALMATIAN FACTS

Dalmatian puppies are born with white, spotless fur. Their spots usually begin to appear within ten days.

Dalmatians can have black or brown spots. The brown ones are called liver spots.

Dalmatians don't just have spots on their fur. They have spots on their skin, toes, nails, and even the insides of their mouths!

Today, Dalmatians are best known as pets, for both families and fire stations, but they once worked for a living. Many years ago, as "fire dogs," they would run in front of horse-drawn fire trucks to clear the way of people.

Even earlier, they worked as "coach dogs." They would run alongside horse-drawn carriages to protect against roadside bandits.

Next up . . .

GUINNESS THE GOOD GIRL GOES TO SCHOOL

Edited by Tracy C. Gold
Illustrations and Initial Book Design by Penny Weber
Final Book Design by Ryan Webb

Published by Guinness the Good Girl LLC.

ISBN: 978-1-961352-05-6

GUINNESSTHEGOODGIRL.COM

Guinness
the Good Girl™

www.ingramcontent.com/pod-product-compliance
Lightning Source LLC
Chambersburg PA
CBHW042124040426
42450CB00002B/57